T0208809

The community church I attended during my Childhood.

My Valley Experience

Beating the Odds

Gertrude Flynn-White

author**HOUSE**®

AuthorHouse™
1663 Liberty Drive
Bloomington, IN 47403
www.authorhouse.com
Phone: 1 (800) 839-8640

Published by AuthorHouse 04/18/2019

ISBN: 978-1-7283-0872-2 (sc)
ISBN: 978-1-7283-0870-8 (hc)
ISBN: 978-1-7283-0871-5 (e)

Library of Congress Control Number: 2019904468

Print information available on the last page.

Contents

DEDICATION

I dedicate this book to my grandchildren who, through their smiles, laughter and playful gestures, provided strength in their own way. They are the little angels God sent to cheer me along the most recent highways and byways on my journey through the valley. They have given me the pleasure that any grandmother would want to enjoy.
I love you.

ACKNOWLEDGMENTS

God smiles when we continually praise and give Him thanks for His blessings. I want to thank Him for affording me the strength, motivation and courage to share my story. I thank my family and friends who provided moral support during the difficult periods of my life. Special thanks to those who catered to my needs in various ways. You all were my daily inspiration. Thanks to all my wonderful prayer partners who, through their continuous prayers, helped to break down barriers and tear down strongholds. Thank you, my dear readers, for reading this book. The writing of this book has allowed me to dig deeper into the mysteries of God and I felt his love, His peace and enjoyed His presence. As you read, I hope this book will do the same for you. God bless you.

PROLOGUE

*M*y Valley Experience is the first book I wrote after God rescued me from unforeseen circumstances which negatively impacted my life. For several months, I ignored the idea of sharing my story as a testimony of God's unconditional love toward me because I didn't want to invite people into my private life by speaking too candidly. As the overwhelming urge intensified, I decided to stop resisting and ask God for direction so that it would be done according to His will.

I have always lived a private life, so I had a conversation with a close family member who encouraged me to share my inspirational blogs on social media. I thought this was a good idea; so I created a Facebook page and shared prayers, inspirational thoughts, scriptures and songs. Then I created a group where persons share similar material. This group grew rapidly and is still doing well. Having done all this, I felt satisfied that I did what God wanted me to do but it was obvious that He wanted more. I started having weird dreams of making presentations in different forums.

One night as I cuddled in bed, I had a soul-stirring dream that frightened me. *In my dream, I knelt on the ground and was creating a large colourful banner. I laboured on it until it was completed. Then I held it up to examine it. Suddenly, a strong wind blew it out of my hands, and it mounted across the sky like a kite. As I watched it move away into the clouds, I stood and admired its beauty. Then some birds started flying around it. They continued moving around the banner until it disappeared into the clouds.* I shared this dream with people in my circle; and some ridiculed me, thinking that my faculties were now dysfunctional. As

I tried to figure out its meaning, the idea of writing an inspirational book became more pronounced, and I began to document events as I remembered them. I started the manuscript and stopped because the unpleasant memories got me too emotional.

I finally decided to embark on a 3-day dry fast for more spiritual empowerment. At the end of that fast, I went back to my manuscript and completed it without fear. Now I can say, "The book is written, and I have shared my story by the leading of the Holy Spirit to inspire those who may have had similar experiences." I hope it will channel the thoughts of the readers to the path that is sure to lead them to permanent restoration and peace of mind. Keep going forward. Each step may get harder, but don't stop. The view is beautiful at the top.

For those who have never had a valley experience before, I implore you to take a closer walk with God so that He will guide and protect you as you continue your journey. You can pass through the valley and find contentment when you dwell in the house of the LORD, where you can feel His presence near you.

As you read the pages of this book, may you find comfort knowing that when you call, He answers; when you ask, He gives; and if you knock, He will open to receive you. He is ever-present, but He doesn't go where He is not invited. I encourage you to trust Him and everything will be all right.

BEING AT PEACE

Life is a journey that is paved with opportunities, successes, setbacks, sickness, disappointments, and other types of adversities. We are faced with challenges on a daily basis, but we can have peace in the midst of a churning world. We can enjoy peace of mind in different ways. Some find it in security, shelter, food and money. Others say it's all about what we do. Marcus Aurelius believed that "He who lives in harmony with himself lives in harmony with the world."

Our thought process and the way we interpret the things that are happening around us create the whirling that so often causes anxiety. We can experience peace and contentment amid the chaos if we control the way we think by allowing the peace of God to guard our hearts and minds. This peace can only be accomplished by being positive and praying consistently instead of worrying about the circumstances around us.

There are many scripture verses that point us to obtaining peace in the midst of life's struggles. God promises us that His peace that transcends all understanding will guard our hearts and our minds in Christ Jesus. He wants that peace to rule in our hearts so that we will be able to deal effectively with the challenging experiences in life. This peace is one of the nine characteristics of the fruit of the spirit, and it breeds contentment. Contentment is the key to unlock the door to our peace of mind. We can access this key through our daily communication with God. The word of God tells us that godliness with contentment is great gain. For we brought nothing into this world, and we can take nothing out of it (1 Timothy 6:6-7) (NIV).

We should be contented with whatever state we find ourselves in. When we are overcome with anxiety and fear, we need to find a quiet place where we can meditate on God's word. This is accomplished by sitting quietly, avoiding distractions, reading scripture verses, listening to the appropriate music, praying and just worshiping God. God wants us to be at peace with ourselves so that we can abide in His presence. He wants us to live a peaceful, accomplished life.

I can truly say that the world didn't give me this peace that I have, and the world can't take it from me. I experience contentment when, like Reinhold Niebuhr, I ask God to "Grant me the serenity to accept the things I cannot change, the courage to change the things I can, and the wisdom to know the difference." My reasoning is not always perfect, but I believe God's word is perfect, containing everything that is necessary to enhance my spiritual life. God's love is unconditional and has no boundaries.

David confirmed this when he said, "Your love, O LORD, reaches to the heavens, Your faithfulness to the skies" (Psalm 36:5) (NIV). God's steadfast love never ceases, and His mercies never end. He is faithful and merciful; so He will not allow us to be tempted, tried or suffer beyond our ability to survive because He always provides a way of escape or the means to endure tribulation. Life is never easy; but for those who love God, "We know that all things work together for good to them that love God, to them who are called according to His purpose. (Romans 8:28) (KJV). I am encouraged by the scripture in Deuteronomy 7:9 (KJV) which reminds us that God is faithful to keep His covenant of love to a thousand generations of those who love Him and keep His commandments. He abides with those who believe in Him and give them inner peace.

Prayer

Heavenly Father, I thank you for Your abundant love, Your grace and Your mercy. Thank You for peace of mind. Thank You for Your faithfulness, even when we fail to be faithful to You. I pray that You will remove anxiety and replace it with the courage to move ahead each day in spite of our circumstances. As we journey through life, may You guide our path and let Your peace reign among us in our family, in our various institutions, in our business places, and even in our churches. Give us clarity of mind to understand Your word. Help us to realize the real purpose for which we were created. Remove every stressful situation from our lives and give us wisdom to deal with the challenges of this life. Grant us Your peace. In Jesus' name, amen.

ROOTED AND GROUNDED

We have no control over how our journey in life begins or ends. We make plans and try to implement them; but the LORD declares that He knows the plan He has for us, plans to prosper us and not to harm us, plans to give us hope and a future (Jeremiah 29:11). (NIV)

We usually start life's journey with a mission we aim to fulfil, but are often encompassed by clouds of doubt and adversity. A successful person is one who ensures that a firm foundation is in place from the outset. In Psalm 1, we are likened to a tree planted by the rivers of water, that bears good fruit in its season, whose leaves will not wither and whatever he does shall prosper. The words of Jeremiah 17:7-8 tells us that the one who trusts in the LORD and has confidence in Him will be blessed. He will be like a tree planted by the water that sends out its roots by the stream. It does not fear when heat comes; its leaves are always green. It has no worries in a year of drought, and never fails to bear fruit. A productive tree that bears much fruit is one whose roots are grounded. The Bible declares in Colossians 2:7 that we should be rooted and built up in Him, and established in the faith as we have been taught, abounding with thanksgiving. When we are rooted and grounded in God's word, we begin life's journey as a good seed planted in fertile soil (Ephesians 3:17).

There is much assurance in these scriptures that we should have a firm foundation in order to survive the perils on our journey.

I can identify with this situation because on my journey, I have encountered many challenges and fought many battles. There were times when I felt like giving up, not being able to understand why I was born in a Christian home, baptized when I was nine years old, grew up in church and still encountered so many challenges. The scripture passages I learned as a child resonated with me throughout my journey; and I often reflect on them for comfort, guidance, direction and protection. We should not allow our present circumstances to determine our future endeavours. When our roots grow deep into the soil, we are better able to survive any season of drought. Every seed that is planted has the potential to grow and produce. However, the output is contingent on the input.

SUNRISE IN CEDAR VALLEY

As I turn around to look at the long, winding road behind me, the one I call my past, I remember the humble beginnings of my parents' home, located in the remote community of Cedar Valley on the lush green hills of Jamaica. My parents raised me with my other siblings in a protective, God-fearing environment. They were poor and hardworking, but very independent. They believed in what the scripture says about training up their children in the way they should go, so that even when they are old, they would not turn from it.

My parents wanted us to have a better life than the one they had, so from an early age, they instilled certain values and attitudes in us. They believed in setting high standards for us as the hills surrounding our community and the vast landscape of farm lands did not define our future. They were serious about our education; but maintained a balance between school, leisure and church. They ensured that homework was completed each evening. We had to recite our poems, learn the patriotic songs and, at the same time, study our Bible verses. We had to say our prayers before we went to bed, and again when we woke up in the mornings. We couldn't eat our meals without saying our 'grace', as they often called it.

Even when we accompanied Dad to his farm, we had to recite scriptures like Psalm 1, Psalm 100, Psalm 23 and 24 (among others) as we climbed the rugged terrain. We walked behind him on his donkey, either singing religious songs or repeating scripture passages. Whenever he rode his mule, he would allow us to ride with him. We enjoyed that experience very much. The words of Deuteronomy 6 were instilled in us from an early age, with verse 7 being a point of focus daily. It states, "Impress them on your children. Talk about them when you sit at home and when you walk along the road, when you lie down and when you get up." As a child, my mother taught us the scripture, "Honour thy father and mother, so that you may live long in the land the LORD your God is giving you." She would roll her eyes and ask us to repeat it whenever she thought we were disobedient or disrespectful.

I remember that my innate potential as a teacher manifested itself in my early life. During recess at the Prickly Pole All-Age School which I attended, I would pretend that I was the teacher, and my classmates were my students. This is where I displayed all the characteristics of my class teacher. When I reached fourth grade, my teacher asked my father to move me from that school because I was ahead of my class and she saw where I had great potential. It did not take much to convince him, and he immediately enrolled me at the Claremont All-Age School which was approximately ten miles away. Now I was the little country girl coming to town, as this was the main town or shopping area for several surrounding communities. It was not convenient to travel daily as public transportation was scarce. So I had the experience of boarding from I was about ten years old. I hardly missed home, as I lived with a couple who had no other child in their home at the time and were generous people. This relocation did not affect my spiritual well-being as I always attended church with them. My parents had a grocery shop that served the community, and my father was a farmer as well as a baker. I always looked forward to coming home on weekends to help them in the shop, sew, or bake products for sale.

After a few years, I joined my siblings who were now attending Shiloh High School which was a private school. Mom and Dad were often criticized for doing this, but they believed in what Malcolm X said about education: "Education is the passport to the future, for tomorrow belongs to those who prepare for it today." I thank them for facilitating that process. If they had allowed poverty to limit their ability to educate their children, my siblings and I would not have accomplished the goals that we set early in life.

My academic pursuits quickly grew and blossomed as I went through primary, secondary, and tertiary institutions; and did well. My mantra was always, "I can do all things through Christ who strengthens me." I did not worry about what others thought of me, and I did not let their opinions define my future. I believed that if I put my trust in God with all my heart, leaned not on my own understanding, and submitted to Him in all my ways, He would direct my path. This belief cemented my spiritual relationship with God as I journeyed from childhood to adolescence and adulthood. It also created and maintained checks and balances in my spiritual and temporal life. Although I was engaged in community projects, I was also active in church, serving as a Sunday School teacher, Youth Director, and Women's Missionary Leader.

It was sometimes challenging to grow up and maintain my Christian principles, but my love for church allowed me to serve God relentlessly and helped me to mature into a modest young lady. My peers sometimes thought I was weird, as I was more attached to the older women in my community than to my teenage group. Unlike my younger siblings, I didn't have many friends; my parents were strict and overprotective of me. I looked forward to coming home on weekends, but the fear of being grounded at home for no apparent reason while my other siblings were allowed to go out with their friends haunted me. However, I can't complain much as this practice helped to keep me sober and focused. I was an avid reader so, being alone at home most times, I found comfort in reading books and magazines. My mother was a seamstress so when I wasn't reading, I was sitting beside her at the sewing machine, waiting to thread the needle each time she needed that to be done. I soon learned the art of sewing and made my mother proud when I made my first high school uniform. Soon after, I was sewing or repairing clothing for my other siblings. My mother always bragged about my sewing skills and some months later, some ladies in my community brought fabric for me to sew their dresses.

From an early age, I learnt that in order to succeed in life, I would have to be prepared to tear down barriers and remove unnecessary boundaries around me. I did not allow my humble beginnings to define my destiny. Instead, I was constantly reminded of this particular song from Veggie Tales, "I am a promise, I am a possibility" and from an early age I tried to set goals and worked assiduously toward accomplishing them.

I will always remember these childhood years as they helped to mold me into the strong, productive woman I am today. I often wish my parents were here to see the mature fruits of the tree they had planted years ago, but they have gone ahead of me, so may their souls rest in peace and light perpetually shine upon them.

Prayer

Heavenly Father, I thank You for the moon that shines in the dark, and for the sun that rises each morning. Its radiance lights up the world around us and reminds us that You are in control of the universe. As it rises, let new hope rise in me. Let Your love shine around me and give me peace. Order my steps that as I grow older each day, I'll be what You want me to be. LORD, give me the courage to pursue the things that will please You and satisfy my needs according to Your will. I thank You for my humble beginning as it taught me to appreciate the things I cannot change. I surrender my all to You and pray that Your Holy Spirit will transform me as I keep my heart and mind focused on You. In Jesus' name, amen.

THE PLANT BLOOMS

While growing up, I was more of an introvert, but that did not limit my involvement in church activities. During my early teens, my church had street meetings in several adjoining communities, and I was always on the agenda to give a testimony or an exaltation. I completed this task with great pride and joy. I bloomed like a flower in a garden, and I knew then that God had destined me for greatness.

I was at church one Sunday when the Parish Overseer visited and the moderator asked me to give an exaltation (this is usually done before the preacher gives the sermon). My focus text was, "For I am persuaded, that neither death, nor life, nor angels, nor principalities, nor power, nor things present, nor things to come, nor height, nor depth, nor any other creature, shall be able to separate us from the love of God, which is in Christ Jesus our LORD." (Romans 8:38-39) (KJV) After I finished speaking, the Bishop, who was the day's preacher, remarked that I was very brave to have made such a strong statement. I didn't quite understand what he meant until several years later, when I faced adversity and had no other choice but to continue believing in God for deliverance.

MAKING GOOD CHOICES

Life is made up of unlimited choices. Sometimes, we have to make decisions that will change our lives forever. One of my attributes is that I don't make decisions without praying about them, regardless of how small they are. This habit has stuck with me on my journey. Another inherent quality is not being afraid of taking calculated risks. I may procrastinate in fear of making the wrong decision, but after I pray about it, I always feel confident that God will let His will be done. It was Stephen Covey who said, "We are the creative force of our life, and through our own decisions rather than our own conditions, if we carefully learn to do certain things, we can accomplish those goals." I have made mistakes, but I try to learn some lessons from them so they are not repeated.

There are some choices that we have to make, no matter how difficult the consequences are, because they determine our destiny. Yet God gives us options when we exercise our faith in Him. We have to listen closely to His direction and be able to determine if He is the voice speaking, as there are many voices. The scripture says, "Have I commanded you? Be strong and courageous. Do not be afraid; do not be discouraged, for the LORD your God will be with you wherever you go." (Joshua 1:9)(NIV)

After I was successful in the first set of exams that would qualify me for tertiary-level education, my parents decided they could no longer afford to send me to school because there were three younger siblings attending the same private school. I was devastated, but at this point in my life, I had absolutely no intention of staying home. So, I prayed for God's direction, and the answer came when I travelled to a nearby community to ask the principal of a primary school if he would allow me to visit that institution for a few hours each week to observe the teachers. When he heard that my reason for doing this was because my parents could not afford to send me back to school, he asked me how far I had reached in school. Then he informed me that I was already qualified to be employed as a pre-trained teacher. I could not believe I was hearing right, but realized he was serious when he asked me to complete the application process. This landed me my first job as a teacher.

I worked for two years before going to college, but this was a hard decision to make because I wasn't sure I would have enough money to take me through the first two years. However, after praying about it, I worked and saved as much as possible, believing that all things work together for good for those who are called according to God's purpose.

As I journeyed through my early teens, I was smart, talented and cute, so there were many guys who liked me and tried to get my attention. Some got it when they called to me and I responded with a smile, although I had to constantly look over my shoulders for my Dad's watchful eyes. I had already welcomed my eighteenth birthday, but I still couldn't be seen talking to the young men in the community out of the norm. However, I was busy in church, so that didn't bother me.

Austin was a young man in my church who was madly in love with me, but I couldn't return his sentiments because I was afraid of my Dad. Sometimes, we looked at each other from the corner of our eyes and smiled, hoping that nobody saw us. I liked when our eyes met, and I enjoyed sitting near him in church. I knew he loved me; and I soon realized that I loved him, too. We often hoped that we would be placed in the same group so we could be close to each other, but that is the closest that we could get. Those days were different. We could not be seen displaying any sign of intimacy in public. I will honestly say this fatal attraction grew stronger and was noticed by our circle of friends in the church, but it was deemed as nothing serious.

After completing my second year of teaching, I had saved enough money, so I enrolled in teachers' college. It was almost at the end of summer holidays, and my father had somehow loosened his reigns on me. I was allowed to go out without much argument and restriction. So, one day my church brother Austin, and I, planned to meet in the nearby town. That morning, I boarded the only bus that was available to transport people from the community to the town. I was bubbling with excitement and couldn't wait for the bus to reach its destination.

The journey took us about ten miles and I wished he was the other passenger sitting beside me. As soon as the bus reached the town, I could see him eagerly anticipating the bus to stop. As I alighted from the bus, he held my hand, and we walked over to the nearby post office. We stood speechless, only staring at each other for a while. Then he held my hand and, with a smile, said, "Gertrude, will you marry me?"

I couldn't hold back the words "Yes! Yes!" as they escaped from my mouth. I instantly froze because I wasn't expecting this.

Suddenly, I thought of how my father would respond if he ever heard about it. I felt a huge lump in my throat as I watched his smile slowly fade when I said, "I'll be going off to college next week."

He was still holding my hands, and he gently squeezed them. While peering into my eyes, he said, "Gertrude, I love you very much, and I want you to be my wife."

I felt my body melting; and tearfully, I said, "If I got married and ever became pregnant at college, I would have to leave." We stared at each other motionlessly, and I felt the tears running down my face. As he used his soft hands to wipe the tears away, I asked, "Can you wait until I finish college?"

He quickly asked, "How long?" I replied, "Two years."

With tear-filled eyes, he said, "That's a long time to wait, Gertrude."

I know I had hurt his feelings and shattered his dreams of marrying me in a few months; but I was now faced with two choices, and I had to make a decision. This was the first time we ever hugged each other, and at that moment, we weren't concerned about who was watching us. I told him I need some time to pray about it, and he said he could only give me one week. That was enough time for me to pray and wait for God's direction.

We spent the rest of the day at the library, and he watched as I boarded the bus that would take me home. I thought about it on my way home, and felt more tears running. I knew whatever decision I made would hurt one of us, but I was willing to accept what God says I should do.

When I reached home, I went straight to the bedroom I shared with my sisters, and cuddled in bed. I wept uncontrollably under my blanket. "Why did this have to happen now?" and "Will he wait on me?" were the questions I kept asking myself over and over. I remember asking

God to let His will be done in my life. "LORD, I don't know what to do, but let your will be done," I cried.

The next day, I wrote him a long letter telling him how much I loved him, and asked him to wait until I completed the first two years of college. I mailed the letter to him, hoping that by the time he received it, I would have already started college. I went to church that Sunday, but he didn't attend. Two weeks later, I received a letter from him telling me he would wait on me, and I was so happy to hear this.

Then at the end of my first semester at college, he told me that he was going to migrate to the United States of America, but he would never stop loving me. I never saw him again, but he would always send his regards to me via his family members. We went our separate ways, living our separate lives, but our love only went into hibernation for thirty-five years before we met again. The seed of love that was sown when we were in our teens was somewhere waiting to germinate. You will hear the rest of this story in another chapter.

Prayer

—————⸻◦(())◦⸻—————

Heavenly Father, we acknowledge You as our LORD and Saviour. We worship You, for You are King of Kings and LORD of LORDS. You number our hairs and determine our years. You hang the stars in place. You create and You destroy. You raise up and You tear down, You open doors that are shut and You close doors that are open. You are the beginning and the end. We praise your name. Almighty God, You said we should trust You and not depend on our own understanding, so we ask that You help us to make the right decisions, as it is not our decisions but Yours that make a difference in our lives. As we plan, may You order our steps and help us to make the right decision. In Jesus' name, amen.

REAPING THE FRUITS

The beginning of a new era in my life had just begun. I graduated from college; and my humble, busy childhood propelled me to pursue further studies in dressmaking and design, and food and nutrition, in addition to my teaching career. I believed if I were multitasked or multiskilled, I would be on the cutting-edge in a competitive world. Each summer holiday, I completed academic courses for personal development as well as short religious studies for building my spiritual awareness.

My journey continued as I basked in the sunshine on what seemed to be the mountaintop. I got married to another man soon after I left college, and God blessed me with two lovely sons. Everything was going well in both my spiritual and temporal life. Self-actualization was in full gear as I now had a profession, a family, a house and a car; and was still serving God. I worked and studied to further my education, and was now working steadily to achieve my goals. Baking and sewing were my favourite hobbies, so I now had a boutique which offered employment to five seamstresses in addition to my usual baking. Christmas was my peak baking season as I was expected to satisfy my customers with their Christmas cakes.

With this huge workload, I still found time to teach young girls sewing and baking in my church through Girl Guides and 4-H clubs.

As I reminisce, I often wonder how I was able to do so many things, but the Bible tells us that each of us has received a gift and we should use it to serve one another, as good stewards of God's varied grace, based on the gifts each of us has received. (1 Peter 4:10). This was my unique way of giving back to my community. I believe that when God blesses us, we should not keep it to ourselves, but think of creative ways to stir up one another to love and good works. Even when we don't have anything tangible to give, we can encourage others.

Being the leader of the Community Services Ministry at church, I worked with my team in identifying and catering to the needs of the less fortunate. This position created an opportunity for me to serve my community on a larger scale. My hectic job at school demanded much of my time, but I still ensured that God's work was not compromised. The Bible tells us in Colossians 3:23-24 that whatever we do, we should do it enthusiastically as something done for the LORD and not for men, knowing that we will receive a reward of an inheritance from the LORD. As a public officer, I served willingly and freely. I never placed any boundaries on my ability to serve.

In life, we travel on level roads or plains, climb hills or mountains, and bask in the ambiance of the mountaintop until sometimes, without warning, we fall and roll down the side of the hill into the valleys below. Often, it is by our own mistakes, but sometimes it is not. I have made mistakes and had to deal with the consequences. Even when we find ourselves in the valley, we should not place limitations on ourselves, but look to the hills from which all our help comes. We can learn a lot from the life of King David. He was a man after God's own heart, but his human nature caused him to be sinful. Yet despite his struggles, he sought after and glorified God. His determination and great confidence in God's faithfulness, and his desire to give praise and thanks to God, allowed him to rise in strength and fame. In his deep despair, he cried, "I called upon the LORD in distress: The LORD answered me and set me in a large place. The LORD is on my side: I will not fear: What can man do unto me?" (Psalm 118: 5-6) (KJV) We are encouraged to face our challenges with confidence, not give up easily, and put our trust in God.

THE POWER OF PRAYER

Whenever we encounter occasional turbulence on our journey, we often panic, and are likely to move into self-pity. It's hard to control how we react at this stage, but if we believe in God, we should not fear. Instead, believe that God will take us through these moments of distress. David reminds us in Psalm 23:1, "The LORD is my Shepherd, I lack nothing. He makes me lie down in green pastures. He leads me beside still waters, He refreshes my soul... Even though I walk through the darkest valley, I will fear no evil, for you are with me; Your rod and Your staff, they comfort me." (NIV). He continues to assure me that God will prepare a table before me in the presence of my enemies. He anoints my head with oil, and makes my cup run over. His goodness and His mercy will follow me wherever I go. I am always comforted by the thought that He will command His angels to guard me in all my ways and at all times. When I get into my car each morning, I communicate with Him as if He is sitting in the passenger seat. I pray and meditate on the word of God, with the assurance that it is a lamp unto my feet and the light on my path. I feel protected when I do that.

As I continued my journey, I triumphed over many obstacles, but Watchman Nee reminds me that "The Christian experience, from start to finish, is a journey of faith." Helen Keller thinks of life as "either a daring experience or nothing at all." The road to success is not usually pleasant, but instead boring and unpredictable. Many people believe that when the road is difficult and tiresome, it will lead to beautiful things, captivating experiences or rewarding destinations. This might be true, but it takes perseverance and determination to overcome the obstacles along the way. We must travel life's journey with a deep consciousness of God in order to triumph over adversity.

Prayer

Heavenly Father, how excellent is Your name in all the earth. I come before You with a heart of thanksgiving for the blessings You have poured on me. You are compassionate and gracious. You are my stronghold in times of trouble, and my shelter in every storm. You blot out my transgressions and supply my needs. You are able to do immeasurably more than I ever ask or imagine. I worship You, LORD. Draw me closer to You so that I may dwell in Your presence. Help me to work according to Your will without complaining or murmuring so that Your name will be glorified. In Jesus' name, amen.

THE VALLEY OF BACA

David had his own experience of the Valley of Baca, as mentioned in Psalm 84. The word "Baca" means weeping. The Valley of Baca is often referred to as "the Valley of Weeping". It's a valley which symbolizes the difficulty, pain and suffering travelers from Bethlehem to Jerusalem experienced as they journeyed through. It was a dangerous and treacherous place to be in, but they maintained their relationship with God. While passing through, God gave them the supplies they needed. Where they were short of natural supplies to sustain themselves, God provided an abundant supply of water to fill the pools. As we know, water is an important commodity in our lives.

I can imagine how cheerful the weary pilgrims were that after travelling on the dreary road, they were able to refresh themselves from the pools as the rain filled them. They became stronger and stronger. As they travelled, they knew their time in the Valley of Baca was only temporary; and so they moved steadfastly to their destination, the city of God. They constantly asked for God's attention, and He supplied the needs of His people as they asked of Him.

Whether we are Christians or not, we will walk through a valley at some point in our lives. For some, the journey may be long and for others short, depending on the circumstances in which we find ourselves, and how each case is handled. This experience is necessary because it allows us to appreciate the mountain encounter. So, when we have our valley moments, God walks through it with the children of God, and He takes them through the difficult times. He promises that He will never leave us nor forsake us.

I had a brother in my church who had to travel through a volatile community to get to his home on the other side of town. He was always cautious of travelling at nights in a particular section of that community. Whenever he approached the area, he would always ensure that his car doors and windows were locked. Then one night, as he reached the center of the village he dreaded most, his car came to an abrupt stop. Reluctantly and fearfully, he alighted and opened the bonnet to see what was wrong. He soon remembered that he was low on petrol when he left work, and had forgotten to stop at the gas station before heading home. He found himself between a rock and a hard place because his gas tank was now empty and he was at an unsafe location. He quickly called his friends to get him some gas, but they were all afraid of venturing in that community.

He said he panicked for a while, but soon found comfort in singing the hymn "The Lord's My Shepherd," as he sat in the car, peering into the darkness and moving his head in a circular motion to see who was coming in the direction of the car. After a few minutes, he repeated Psalm 91:1-2, which states, "He that dwelleth in the secret place of the most High shall abide under the shadow of the Almighty. I will say of the LORD, He is my refuge and my fortress; my God, in Him will I trust..." He got out of the car, took his personal belongings, and started walking toward home. Each time he heard the sound of a vehicle or footsteps coming, he took cover in the nearby bushes. He had to walk a few miles, but he reached home safely that night. He didn't find any time to worry about his car because he was so tired, he soon fell asleep.

The next day, he bought gas and went back for his car, which was still locked and with everything as he had left them. When he related the incident to his friends, they told him of instances where people were robbed and even shot in that same area.

What lessons have we learned from this story? God is always near us, but we need to get His attention by calling upon Him.

I had my first valley experience when my older son was ten months old. He became ill, and his Dad and I rushed him to the hospital. The doctors and nurses tried their best; but when they told us that they had done all they could, I knew that I had to tap into the supernatural realm. When I looked at my baby, his eyes had turned over and I immediately knew his case was serious. Without thinking, I climbed over into his crib, hugged him and prayed as if I were dying, too. They compelled me to get out of the crib, and as I climbed down, they led me from the room. I continued praying where I stood outside. Later that day, I returned to the ward and saw my baby moving his little hands and feet. I thanked God for His divine intervention as my son moved through recovery. This was my first glimpse of adversity; but God was my refuge and strength, a very present help in times of trouble. I found strength in the words of the LORD as He admonishes us to be strong and courageous, not afraid or discouraged, for He will be with us wherever we go.

When I went back to college for further studies, I came home one evening, and my sons were at my next-door neighbour's house. When my older son, who was about eight years old, heard my voice, he ran from their house toward me, not knowing that their big Alsatian dog was outside his kennel. As he tried to exit the gate, the dog attacked him. At first, I panicked and screamed for help, but no one heard me. The dog had my son on the ground, digging its teeth viciously into his flesh.

By this time, some smaller dogs from the neighbourhood joined the attack, and were jumping around and barking. I found myself fighting desperately to save my son as I cried "Help! Help! Jesus! Jesus!" I grabbed a large stone and hit the dog as he sank his teeth into my son's face. Then I heard the voice of my neighbour's son calling the dog's name. At that moment, the dog released his hold on my son and ran. With the help of my neighbours who had now gathered, we rushed him to the nearby clinic. However, when the nurse on duty examined him, she suggested that we rush him in the ambulance to the hospital.

My son spent the night in hospital, and was released the next day with bandages all over his body. I was still traumatized, but was grateful that his injuries were not life-threatening.

PRAYING IN THE NAME OF JESUS

The name of Jesus is powerful. When we pray, we should pray in the name of Jesus. It is more than just a habit to end our prayers "in the name of Jesus", or "in Jesus' name". This is an acknowledgment of the believer's faith in Jesus Christ, with the understanding that our prayers are heard as we bow before the throne of God. When we pray in the name of Jesus, it means praying according to God's will. We are confident that He listens to our prayers and will respond to our requests when we ask for anything that is in line with His will. The Word of God asks us not to be anxious about anything, but in every situation, by prayer and petition, and with thanksgiving, present our requests to God. As children of God, we should not worry about anything because His peace is with us to guard our hearts and our minds.

I was plunged into another valley when my older son was sixteen years old. He was adept at Mathematics and computer studies, and would often tutor his friends who were preparing for high school exams. When he graduated from high school, he was still too young to enter any tertiary institution, so we enrolled him at a community college where he could complete a pre-university course.

He had just completed his first semester and was excited that he now had time to unwind. During the Christmas holiday, he spent most of his time helping other students with their school projects. He always liked to be around me whenever I was baking, and I welcomed his help in preparing the many fruitcakes I had to supply my customers that Christmas. We were a happy family, but no one knew that was going to be the last Christmas he would ever spend with us.

Prayer

———⫸⫷⫸———

Heavenly Father, I exalt You, for You have been my hiding place, and You allow me to find refuge under Your wings. I look to You because Your love, Your goodness and Your mercy surround me each day. LORD, I put my trust in You so I will not fear what man will do to me. I pray for protection over my family in the name of Jesus. I entrust my children into Your loving care. May You cover them with the blood of Jesus and guard them from temptation. Help them to realize that You are in control of their lives, and their future is in Your hands. Send Your angels to strategic places, ready to protect them from harm. In Jesus' name, amen.

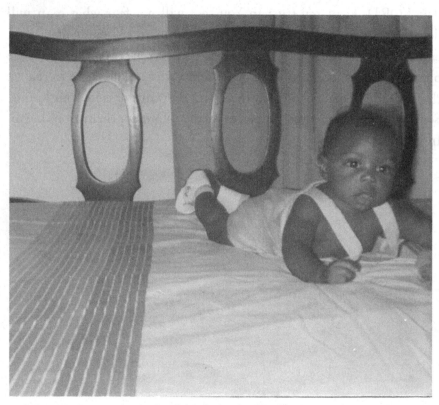

My son Devar was a healthy baby before becoming seriously ill.

THE VALLEY OF WEEPING

O f course, we have good days and bad days. On some days, we rejoice; and on other days, we become sad because of circumstances around us. How many times on your journey are you brought to a place where tears are your only language? What do you do during such difficult periods? Do you bathe in self-pity, or do you look to the hills where your help comes from? Rest assured that God sees the tears of a brokenhearted soul. He even hears them when they fall.

Tears are a language that God understands, so we should weep if we have to do so because crying helps to relieve us from tension or anxiety. However, we should not weep as those who have no hope. This weeping may last for a short period as the God of hope will fill us all with joy and peace in believing so that by the power of the Holy Spirit, we may abound in hope.

This is why we should not become hopeless when we are faced with adversity because if we put our trust in God, it will only be an experience and not a destination.

It is a test of our faith when we find ourselves in adverse situations, but we are certain to receive a blessing if we remain steadfast under trial. For when we have stood the test, we will receive the crown of life, which God has promised to those who love him (James 1:12). It is not easy to overcome the trials, challenges or setbacks we encounter on life's journey; but after we have suffered for a little while, the God of grace will Himself restore, confirm, strengthen and establish us (1 Peter 5:10). The evidence is seen both in our spiritual walk with Him and in our temporal life. Our trials are unique, and may appear anytime and anywhere on our journey. Trouble or any form of adversity is no respecter of anyone or status. It strikes without warning in most cases when we are least prepared, as it did two weeks before my first son's seventeenth birthday.

It was a pleasant Saturday morning and I was going to be one of the judges at my church's Youth Retreat. My husband and I took our younger son with us on an errand early that morning, leaving his brother in bed. On our return, we saw a crowd at our gate. Then one of my neighbours stopped us and asked, "Where is your car?"

"It is parked in my yard, parallel to the fence," I replied.

As we approached the gate, I saw people crying. Some were sitting in the road and on the sidewalk, weeping uncontrollably. I quickly glanced over the concrete fence where I had parked my car that morning to see if it was still parked where I had left it. Unfortunately, it wasn't there. Immediately, I knew something was amiss.

As our vehicle came to a complete stop, my neighbours started crowding around me, expressing sympathy. As soon as we heard that my son was involved in a car accident and was rushed to the hospital, we headed in that direction.

On the way to the hospital, I was too shocked to pray, but I remember asking God to have His way. All I kept saying was, "Have Your way, LORD. Have Your way."

With weakened legs and pain in my voice, I quickly identified myself and asked the nurse at the hospital for my son. She pointed to a room and told us to speak with the doctor. As I entered the room, the doctor offered me a chair and insisted that I sit before he spoke. I just couldn't sit or keep still. I paced the room from side to side, and kept asking the doctor to tell me what happened. I remember asking frantically, "Where is my son? I just want to see my son." Then he asked my husband to try and get me to sit.

Before my husband could touch me, I shouted unintentionally,

"Doctor, whatever you are going to tell me, you will have to tell me while I am standing because I cannot sit."

I guess he read my eyes and realized that I meant what I said. He stood silently for a while, and then he said to both of us, "Come with me." I walked anxiously and silently beside him to a room in the waiting area of the hospital.

He paused before opening the door, then ushered us into a room where my son was lying on the bed. My son lay on his back and appeared to be sleeping. We rushed over to the bed; and I shouted my son's name, hoping that the loud sound of my voice would wake him up. He didn't move, so I shook him, but he still didn't move. I shouted his name several times, but there was no response.

Then I heard a low voice from behind me:

"He didn't survive."

I quickly turned around and realized that it was the voice of the doctor, who had not left the room. I hugged my son's helpless body, buried my face in his stomach, and wept uncontrollably. By this time, my younger son, who was sitting on a chair in the hallway, heard me screaming and entered the room. Immediately, I was plunged into a different world: "the Valley of Weeping".

As we left the hospital, I tried to reminisce as best I could on the sequence of events that morning. I remembered that the day before the accident, my son gave his room an unusually deep cleaning, including changing around furniture. I was amazed, but praised him anyhow. That Saturday morning, as I got dressed, it was unusual for him to be playing with me so much. He told me to drive my car, but I wanted to save on gas, so I told him I would rather have his father drive his pickup truck.

Then he asked me to change the dress that I was wearing. When I asked if he had a reason, he said, "Too much flowers, Mommy." I was shocked when I realized that he went for one of his t-shirts and insisted that I wear it instead. It was not suitable for the event I was attending, but I found myself slipping it over my head reluctantly, just to appease him. I planned to change it when I returned from the event. Did he sense that he was going to leave me? I can't tell, but I still have his t- shirt.

His death was a shock to the entire community. I was totally devastated, and wondered why God had allowed it to happen. I felt like giving up on God because He had let me down. I was angry at my son for allowing his friend to influence him to take my car for a ride, knowing quite well that he was not a driver. I kept the car keys in a safe place where no one would have access to it, and I was sure my children would never find them. I couldn't understand why God allowed this incident to happen while He was still in control of my son's life. I know God could have saved him.

The car my son was driving collided with another vehicle, and the driver spent several months recovering in hospital. It was rumoured that we would have to sell all our possessions to pay the liabilities. While I was mourning his loss, I had to think of the consequences. We had a life insurance policy for him, but we were denied the benefits because he wasn't a licensed driver.

A few months after his funeral, I was visited by one of my cousins who lived in England. I was so happy to see her, but this feeling soon turned to despair when she told me that she had come to purchase my house after hearing that we would have to sell it to pay for damages incurred by the accident. I bravely told her that even

if this was going to happen, the time had not come yet. So my husband showed her some other properties listed on the mPaargkee|t.33I share this incident because when we are experiencing distress, the persons we expect to offer us moral support are sometimes the ones who cause us more hurt. This was the most difficult period in my life.

During this dilemma, we were slapped with a lawsuit of millions of dollars resulting from my son's death, but God has a way of fighting our battles for us when we put our trust in Him. I had a strong belief that if we prayed earnestly, God would answer our prayer and subsequently deliver us. Again, with prayer and supplication, we made our request known to God, and His supernatural intervention was manifested as every Goliath that stood up against us fell. I was now confident that God was still in control and would lead us through this period of despair.

"We may be hard pressed on every side, but not crushed; perplexed, but not driven to despair; persecuted, but not forsaken; struck down, but not destroyed." (2 Corinthians 4:8-9) When we find strength to worship God in the face of adversity and praise Him for every battle fought and won, He will restore, confirm, strengthen, and establish us. God moves in a mysterious way and will do everything according to His will and His own timing. He also promises that He will fight for you but you need only to be still (Exodus 14:14) NIV.

I remembered what my Bishop had said after I gave that exaltation at church, and I thought about it for a while: "Nothing can separate me from God's love… neither death nor life…" During the period of bereavement, this scripture lingered in my mind and as I reflected on it, I realized that my faith in God is being tested. For a while, I was haunted by the question, "Can the death of a loved one separate me from the love of God?" The answer to that is "No! Nothingshould."

As I mourned his passing, I realized that I was no longer basking in the atmosphere of the mountaintop, but was plunged into the bottom of a deep valley — a dark dungeon. Yet I was determined to continue trusting God. I soon found solace in David's prayer in Psalm 61:1-4:

"Hear my cry O God; attend unto my prayer. From the end of the earth will I cry unto thee, when my heart is overwhelmed: lead me to the rock that is higher than I. For thou hast been a shelter for me, and a strong tower from the enemy. I will abide in thy tabernacle forever. I will trust in the cover of thy wings."(KJV)

After reading this scripture, I sang the lyrics version of it daily. There were several persons who prayed for us and with us. I believed that God would keep His promise to be with us when we pass through the waters. When we pass through the rivers, He will not let them sweep over us. When we walk through the fire, He will not allow it to burn us, and the flames will not set us ablaze. Surprisingly, in the midst of despair, my faith grew stronger. I knew I had to be strong for the other members of my family, and I could only get that strength from the Almighty God.

LIGHT SHINES OUT OF DARKNESS

To us, difficult times are like dark clouds that pass overhead and block the beautiful sunlight from the plants that depend on it for their existence. It is hard to say this, but we should not become hopeless because of devastating circumstances. The saying "Beyond every dark cloud, there is a silver lining" comes to my mind when I reflect on the sequence of events that followed my period of bereavement. Looking back, I realize that in spite of the traumatic experiences that engulfed my little world like a whirlwind, God's plan was not complete. Sometimes, when we think we have been through so much that nothing worthwhile is left of us, God steps in and proves us wrong. That is the time He is ready to raise us up so we can climb mountains. That is the time He raises us up so we can walk with Him on stormy seas. We will remain strong when we abide with Him. When He takes us through the storm, he readily prepares a table for us in the presence of our enemies and fills our cup until it overflows.

Three months after my son died, my friend Andrew visited my house to use my computer to apply for a teaching job in the United States. After uploading his application, he encouraged me to submit my application too because it would provide an opportunity for me to take a break from my immediate environment. I was reluctant at first, but after researching the programme, I realized that my entire family would be able to migrate. I still did not think I was mentally ready for this type of transition, but I reluctantly uploaded my application.

A few days after, both of us were informed of our acceptance in the programme. We were so excited to know that within a few months, we would be teaching in another country, and we would have our families with us. As the days moved by quickly, we moved smoothly through the various stages of recruitment.

I almost withdrew from the programme when my husband indicated that he was no longer interested in leaving Jamaica. At first, I was confused, but as I prayed about it, my faith grew stronger, and I finally decided to go. At the end of five months, we relocated to the United States and were actively blending in with the American education culture. This was a rewarding experience for my son and me. We remained a close-knit family. My son and I visited home during school breaks while his father visited us regularly. However, there is an old Jamaican proverb: "There are many slips between the cup and the lip." This means that even when a good outcome or positive result seems certain, things can go wrong.

During a short school break, I decided to visit home unannounced. Instead of the usual airport pickup, I rented a car. My son and I drove all the way from the airport to our home. It did not take long for me to realize that something was amiss. I couldn't immediately put the pieces of the puzzle together, but what the eyes could behold was enough to convince anyone that our marriage was under attack. My loving husband of many years had changed so much. The skeleton in the closet refused to remain hidden and paraded without any remorse.

Much effort was made to resolve the issues, but the spirit of Jezebel was hard at work and would do anything and everything to tear us apart. It eventually moved beyond reconciliation; and after praying earnestly without any eminent resolution in sight, I walked away gracefully. Thank God for the strength He has given me to beat the odds. Today, I hold no grudge against anyone, and I have no regrets concerning the choices I made. They were the right decisions at the right time, and I praise God for the wisdom to act when I had to do so. God has blessed me and has restored me sevenfold. Sometimes, adversity knocks us out of our comfort zone; but as painful as it is, God will restore us if we trust Him.

My time spent in the United States was the silver lining I spoke of earlier; the experience and knowledge gained created the knowledge-based foundation for greater opportunities that came later.

WHEN IT RAINS, IT POURS

"When it rains, it pours" or "It never rains but it pours" are two idiomatic expressions that were designed to be positive, but people have frequently used them with a negative connotation. I borrow these expressions to emphasize the fact that sometimes, when troubles or problems appear, they come one after another. I continued my journey through life, being faithful to God despite my pitfalls. I remained cognizant of the potential battles and battlegrounds of spiritual warfare; and the need to be in a constant relationship with God, where His protection is guaranteed.

It's hard to believe that the loss of a loved one gets easier as time goes by. Not when death leaves scars that seem impossible to be healed by anyone. It was Jonathan Harnisch who said, "Sadly enough, the most painful goodbyes are the ones that are left unsaid and never explained." This reminds me of my two brothers who became ill and were admitted to separate hospitals which were many miles apart. My youngest brother, Errol, suddenly started having multiple seizures, and remained in hospital for observation. He underwent a series of tests, but there was no clear diagnosis of the causes. While this was going on, my older brother, Harry, was undergoing a major surgery. It was successfully done, but his health deteriorated rapidly afterward.

We were making arrangements for Errol to do another medical evaluation when we received the sad news of his death. The following day, family members visited Harry at the other hospital, but they were greeted with the news that he had died as well. It is never easy to deal with the death of one family member, and here we were forced to absorb the reality of two brothers dying a day apart. Our parents predeceased them, and as usual, my siblings expected me to be in charge of funeral arrangements. I was living in the United States at that time, and had to do most of the planning and organizing on the phone. This was not an easy task, as we were often too emotional to speak.

The day of the funeral was a solemn one not only for the family, but for the community as this was going to be the first double funeral ever held there. It wasn't easy, sitting in that church staring at two caskets, knowing that the persons inside were my two brothers. However, God provided strength in our weakness and comfort in our moments of despair.

Many people are paranoid about death and are reluctant to talk about it. I might sound morbid, but I used to be like those people who are afraid of having a conversation about this subject. I saw death as an enemy who appears unannounced. But I am comforted by the words, "To everything there is a season, and a time to every purpose under the heaven: A time to be born, and a time to die; a time to plant, and a time to pluck up that which is planted; a time to kill, and a time to heal; a time to break down, and a time to build up." Ecclesiastes 3:1-3 (KJV).

One of the lessons I have learnt here, is that we should always find time to express sentiments of love, affection and appreciation to our family. Some people are fortunate to be around their loved ones when they take their last breath. This is a special moment of awe when the soul is about to return to God. Some sing their favourite hymns, or repeat their favourite Bible verse, or they may even make their final request. We must always remember that no matter how overwhelmed we are with grief, God still walks beside us. He will guide us and give us strength.

THE POTTER'S CLAY

The Bible tells us that our LORD is the potter, we are the clay, and we all are the work of His hand. Sometimes, God sees cracks or faults in His creation, and chooses to take us back to the potter's house. This is an important process that He wanted the prophet Jeremiah to see. The LORD instructed Jeremiah to go down to the potter's house so he could hear the words of the LORD. When he reached the house, he saw the potter working at the wheel, shaping the clay. The LORD wanted Jeremiah to see the potter working with the clay at the wheel so he could understand the different stages in the process before He spoke to him.

He noticed the preparation of the clay as it was being dug from the soil. He observed the molding and strengthening of the clay, and realized the purpose of the clay. As Jeremiah watched, the LORD asked him, "Can I not do this with you, Israel, as this potter does?"

Like clay in the hand of the potter, so are we in God's hand. He can uproot and tear us down when we disobey Him, and rebuild us when we repent. God was speaking about the disobedience of Israel, who He had delivered from bondage in Egypt. He has a unique way of reprimanding His children. Where does God see us? Are we on the potter's wheel? Or are we going through the furnace? What is our purpose? Are we fulfilling that purpose? Are we being used as a vessel of honour?

Let us imagine ourselves in God's hands being molded as the potter's clay; He created us into His likeness but He constantly molds us over and over again so that we can become a vessel of honour for His will to be done in our lives.

The process is often painful, but when God is finished with us, we are like fine gold.

The scripture tells us in James 1:2-8, "My brethren, count it all joy when you fall into various trials, knowing that the testing of your faith produces patience. But let patience have its perfect work, that you may be perfect and complete, lacking nothing." (NKJV) It is not easy for us to go through tribulations and still worship God in spirit and in truth, but He promises that He will wipe away all the tears from our eyes.

There will be no more pain, no more sorrow, no more crying for the former things are passed away.

I continue to serve both my church and community in different capacities, but I still rely on God's lead. I try as best as I can to keep on the full armor of God so that I can take a stand against the schemes of the devil. After much reflection and introspection, I realize that for those who love God, all things work together for good for those who are called according to his purpose. In many cases, we don't know our purpose, but God is constantly saving us for a reason. Therefore, we should ask Him to fulfil His purpose in us.

Prayer

———⟨⟨◉⟩⟩———

Heavenly Father, I exalt Your Holy name. I thank You for lifting me from the depths of the valley. Thank You for saving me from my enemies. You healed my broken heart and made my royal mountain stand firm. You turned my mourning into dancing. You removed my sackcloth and clothed me with grace. So many times, the enemy tried to rob me of my joy, but my hope is built on nothing less than the blood of Jesus and His righteousness. I will not fear what man can do to me because my strength is in You. I will praise You forever. May You fulfil the purpose for which You have saved me, and may you continue to guide my steps. In Jesus' name.

My son Devar before he was mauled by my neighbour's dog.

Sitting with my two sons, Devar and his younger brother.

PROCLAIMING HIS GOODNESS

I t is important and highly recommended that as Christians, we share our testimony when God blesses us or delivers us. Testimonies encourage others and build their faith. Many of us, including myself, often shy away from this because we try to live a private life. God smiles when we give Him thanks and praise for His goodness. Jesus says if we acknowledge Him before men, He will acknowledge us before His father who is in Heaven. David was always thankful to God, and we can see this in the Psalms. In some scriptures, he thanked God for His goodness, His steadfast love that endures forever, and for delivering him from trouble.

The Samaritan woman went away evangelizing after she met Jesus. She told people that she had met a man who knew everything about her. This resulted in them coming to meet the man Jesus for themselves. Her simple testimony of what she had experienced led others to meet the Saviour of the world. People generally love to hear stories; but in telling these stories, we should share experiences that inspire others.

I was at church one Saturday afternoon at the start of a one-week revival. During testimony service, the urge came to walk up to the front, take the microphone, and share my testimony. I looked around and thought I left my painful past behind me, and didn't want to rehash any memories of it. The seat became hot and I was now restless. I turned to one of my church sisters and told her what was happening. She said I should go and whatever the LORD wanted the brethren to hear, that's what He will allow me to say. I jokingly said to her, "My book has too many pages, so I don't know which one God would want me to open."

As I tried to make up my mind, the seat became unbearably hot, and I knew I had to go. So I slowly walked to the front, and took the microphone from Pastor. He smiled surprisingly and encouragingly at me as I began to speak.

Before I returned to my seat, my brethren walked up to me, hugged me and commended me for how candidly I spoke. I remember one young lady saying, "Sister, you don't look like any of that ever happened to you. We see you at church every week, looking so pleasant, and had no clue that you had those experiences."

I did not know that God was about to favour me with a big promotion at my job the Thursday of that same week, a promotion that took me up to my retirement.

FULFILLING HIS PURPOSE

Promotion comes from God alone. Only God can fulfil our purpose because He alone knows the plan He has for us. He alone opens doors that no one can shut. He also shuts doors that no one can open. It is always good to humble ourselves under the mighty hand of God, that He may exalt us in due time. When He is ready, He will make us the head and not the tail without making us aware of what is happening. Soon after I testified of His goodness, God was about to promote me, and I found myself resisting an opportunity to serve.

The summer holidays had just ended, and preparations for the reopening of school for the new school year were in high gear. The school's Board of Management asked me to assume the position of acting principal and without thinking, I declined. My immediate response was, "Why me and not another?" I knew that I don't make major decisions without praying about them first, but that was not going to be accepted as an excuse now. I was pressured and confused as there were other tenured persons there who could fill that position. I wondered why they declined, and I kept asking God "Why me? Why this time?"

I worked in my classroom that day and quietly communed with God because I really wanted to make the right choice. I questioned Him and listened for answers, but the answer never came the way I had expected. Then I reflected on the scripture that states, "For promotion cometh neither from the east, nor from the west, nor from the south. But God is the judge: He putteth down one, and setteth up another," Psalm 75:6-7 (KJV)

As I thought about these words, I realized that God was in the midst of this situation. If I accept the position, I would be fulfilling His purpose, and He would be there to guide me. I was consoled by the thought that I would only be acting principal for one month, and this made me accept the position until the principal returned to school.

Traditionally, the school boasted an impressive record of high Common Entrance passes as well as exceptional Grade Six Achievement

Test results annually. Various Scholarships had been awarded to students both in academics and extra-curricular activities. The school dominated parish and national finals in Spelling Bee, Math, Debating and Essay competitions, quizzes and Sports. It also provided Jamaica with two of its Scripps Howard International Spellers in 1997 and 1998 respectively. Now the tides had turned and the baton was placed in my hand to continue the race. Questions began to flood my mind as I conducted a SWOT analysis of the school. Were others aware of the present state of affairs why they declined when asked to accept the acting position? Will I ever get the others on my team to move the organization to its original state? The answers to these questions were embedded in my strength of character, my ability to lead effectively, and my faith in God.

This was my sixth year at the school and I had been doing my own observations and assessment along the way. As I thought about the expectations of this new position, though temporary, I realized that I had to present my Action Plan to my superiors as soon as possible. Much work needed to be done to the infrastructure especially the Grade Four Block that housed my classroom and three others. My reflections took me back from my first day at this institution to the present, and I remembered that Grade Four teachers as well as students were constantly exposed to the elements of nature. On a sunny day, the single fan in each classroom was no match for the overwhelming heat that penetrated the roof made of zinc without ceiling. On a rainy day, teachers had to set containers at different locations in the classrooms to catch water from the leaking roofs. One day I decided that enough was enough. I was tired of complaining about this major inconvenience so I met with the other seven teachers who occupied the building and suggested that we could draft a letter of complaint to the relevant authorities. They all thought that this was a good idea but no one volunteered to write it for fear of the repercussions that would ensue. I finally took the bold step of writing the letter and getting the others to attach their signatures. Then I forwarded it to the Principal and Board of Management. No action was taken immediately but a few years later the Ministry of Education responded by building a new block with eight classrooms. The academic performance was also a major concern.

As I viewed the present condition, I realized that the school was almost bursting at its seams with an enrolment of over sixteen hundred students and close to sixty teachers. The principal was frequently absent because of illness and the school's leadership which is a critical component in ensuring the overall success of the school had just received an unsatisfactory rating by the most recent assessment of the National Education Inspectorate (NEI). The academic performance of the students had taken a downward trend and the discipline which had once met expectation was now a matter of concern to all stake holders.

It was difficult to identify the leadership styles being employed by the administrators and this complacency had negatively impacted the school's culture. It was evident from the outset that drastic changes would have to be made in implementing the recommendations of the NEI report. Changes in the school's culture was imminent and this would be a bittersweet situation for all parties involved. Every organization has its own unique culture and it is one of the most difficult components to change. In effecting this change, emotional intelligence would play a key role in ensuring that personal and professional success is not compromised. It was also important to create a balance between encouraging teamwork and implementing corrective measures.

This new experience had many unforeseen challenges awaiting me. During the first few months, I experienced pockets of resistance as I found myself surrounded by resentment and opposition. The adversaries tried to use different mediums to overpower or eliminate me but I had the support of teachers, parents, the Board of Management and the Ministry of Education. I believed that when Christ is in the vessel, it gives us the courage to smile at the storm. As an administrator, I lead by example and I was determined to succeed. I used Carlos Rodriguez words, "Tough times don't define you, they refine you." To energize me. My immediate weapon was always, "I plead the blood of Jesus." When "Grace and Favour" came our way, I always shouted "Hallelujah" seven times. I soon became an undercover prayer-warrior, but not many people knew this.

My faith in God was strong; and I believed if God led me to it, He would take me through it, and He did. The Word of God assures us, "And without faith it is impossible to please God: because anyone who comes to Him must believe that He exists, and that He rewards those who earnestly seek Him." Hebrews 11:6 (NIV)

I realized that the road to success is in itself a battlefield, and reliance on the Holy Spirit is of paramount importance. I depended on God for direction, protection, sustenance and perseverance. I had the confidence that God was going to see me through such a time as this. Soon, great things began to happen. The pockets of resistance changed into collaborative forces, and teamwork was eminent everywhere. Success came from different directions. As a team, we broke down barriers and soared to a higher level. Our School Wide Intervention Program designed to address the social, emotional and behavioural needs of the students played a major role in improving disciple throughout the school. God's blessings were new every morning and evident everywhere. The principal had not resumed as he was still out on sick leave and what was meant to be one month had turned into months ending my first year in this new position.

I had just received my Golden Torch Award for having completed thirty-six years in teaching, and was preparing to celebrate a new level of success when tragedy struck. That same day, I was involved in a terrible car accident that almost claimed my life, but God wasn't ready for me to go. Yes, my death sentence was issued by my adversaries, but that was not in God's plan. We need to be strong and courageous. We should not be terrified of our adversaries, for the LORD our God goes with us; He will never leave us nor forsake us. The LORD reminds us that He is faithful, and He will strengthen us and protect us from the evil one. (2 Thessalonians 3:3)

I spent four days in the emergency room because the doctors saw signs of internal bleeding. I express my gratitude to those doctors and nurses who attended to me. It was rumored that I would not survive that accident, but God was busy on the job. People who looked at my totaled car asked if I had come out alive, but the angel of the LORD encamps round about them that fear Him. He is my refuge and strength, an ever- present help in times of trouble. There were no cuts or bruises on my body—only the impression of the seatbelt that held me intact. His word says, "I shall not die, but live, and declare the works of the LORD." (Psalm 118:17) His plan for us is always for good and not evil.

After two weeks, I was discharged from the hospital with no life-threatening injuries. We serve a great, big, wonderful God who is a God of impossibilities. After two months, I returned to school driving an SUV, a bigger vehicle than the one that had crashed. I call this a blessing because in spite of the circumstances, God had moved me to another level. This was evidence of God's unconditional love and His saving grace toward me.

My faith in God grew from strength to strength, and I spoke boldly about His goodness and mercy. I began to do spiritual introspection and retrospection because I knew God has saved my life for a purpose. My prayer was for Him to help me to fulfil that purpose. The story of David and Goliath is one of the Biblical experiences embedded in our language as a metaphor for unexpected victory. It is a constant reminder of what happens when an ordinary person confronts an extraordinary unavoidable situation. So there were other battles that I fought; but each time the enemies came in like a flood, God lifted up a standard against them. I firmly believe that no weapon formed against me shall prosper; and every tongue that rises against me in judgment, through the authority of the Holy Ghost, I have the power to condemn it. (Isaiah 54:17)

Sometimes we are forced to respond to overwhelming challenges and have to resist the temptation to quit. First, we need to understand the dynamics of a power struggle and decide on the most effective yet subtle way to react to it. There are times when we have to decide whether to play by the rules or follow our own instincts. This can be easily accomplished when we allow ourselves to be guided by the Holy Spirit. Then we have to be willing to forgive so that we are not subjective in the decision-making process. Our success is contingent on the way we handle problems or conflicts. As leaders, we are expected to lead by example and sometimes our quiet and rather subdued response comes as a surprise to those who expect us to react the same way we are attacked. Like David, we are more successful when we rely on God's direction.

My tenure moved from temporary to permanent and together my staff and I became a strong team. National Commercial Bank adopted the school and Sandals Foundation along with other corporate groups made tangible donations which helped to boost the intervention programs we implemented to raise the standards. Many prominent persons tried to attach themselves to the school in various ways. Dervan Malcolm, Power 106FM Talk Show Host, aired his radio program, "Both Sides of the Story" live from the school with the Grade sixth students as his panelists and they performed well. Television Jamaica (TVJ) personality, Aunty Susan, filmed the popular "The Susan Show" with students from the school. With the help of a vibrant PTA, contributions from stakeholders from inside and outside the community, the school moved from unsatisfactory to satisfactory within a short period.

Prayer

————)(((●)))(————

Heavenly Father, I praise Your Holy name, for even though You are so high above, You care for the lowly and the proud cannot hide from you. Thank You for moving me to another level, even when I don't deserve it. Forgive me for the times I try to figure out life's journey on my own. You know every decision I am about to make, and every challenge I will face. So LORD, send Your Holy Spirit to strengthen me and direct my footsteps. When I am surrounded by troubles, You keep me safe. You oppose my angry enemies, and You fight my battles and save me by Your power. LORD, Your love is everlasting. May You guide and protect me as I move into the unknown. I pray for wisdom, knowledge and understanding as I face each new day. Complete the work that You have begun in my life. Thank You for all that You have already done, and thank You for what You are about to do. In Jesus' name, amen.

The old Grade 4 block of classrooms

The new Grade 4 block of classrooms

Gertrude being awarded for 36 years of service in teaching.

Gertrude, Principal of Ocho Rios Primary School

THE VALLEY OF ADVERSITY

I lived a single life for many years, and had no intention of changing that status. But Washington Irving's statement, "Love is never lost. If not reciprocated, it will flow back and soften and purify the heart", explains how my life changed when I reunited with my teenage boyfriend, Austin, who had proposed to me years before I went off to college. We hadn't seen each other for over thirty-five years, but after we reunited, we communicated casually for a few years before deciding to continue from where we left off years before. After praying about this new venture, we sealed our youthful love with marriage, and we were happy to be together again.

We often reminisced about the moment he proposed to me, and now we were able to laugh about it together. Sometimes he would tease, "Girl, I waited on you for over thirty-five years, and nobody is going to steal you from me again."

I would just look into his eyes, smile and say, "Never".

We had so much in common. He still loved church, and would often play his guitar as if to serenade me. Both of us were at the peak of our careers, and had accomplished all the goals that we had set earlier. Our lives were now on cruise control as we approached the period of retirement. We had made several plans together and often talked about how romantic we would still be in our old days. We both decided to retire early so we could spend a longer time together.

THE UNFORESEEN SUNSET

Retirement is like a long vacation that I carefully planned for. During my years of hard work, I anticipated the day when I would stop working hard to meet deadlines, retire to bed at my own discretion and wake up without an alarm clock. The long- awaited day had come and it was now one week since I retired. It was a beautiful sunny Friday morning. I woke up early and headed in the direction of my school to sign some cheques as the new set of signatories were not yet finalized. I felt happy and relaxed knowing that this would be a simple task compared to my previous work load.

About a mile from my destination, I encountered a long line of traffic going bumper to bumper in the opposite direction. This usually happens when the cruise ship docks at Reynolds Pier in Ocho Rios. Suddenly, a silver car appeared in my lane, overtaking the long line of traffic and speeding towards me. I began applying my brakes and quickly glanced to my left to see if I could swerve to the soft shoulder but there was not enough space between my car and the sea below. On my right, there was no space for him to pass between the vehicles and my car. The car was just a few chains in front of me and I slammed on the brakes and shouted, "I plead the Blood of Jesus" I didn't see the car again but I found myself still seated in my car which was now going slowly and several vehicles behind me. I continued driving but couldn't stop shouting, Hallelujah! Hallelujah! Hallelujah! I regained my composure and continued on my journey to the school. I slowly alighted from my car and walked into the vice principal's office where both of them greeted me. As I returned the compliment, I couldn't hold back the tears of joy. "I met death at Reynolds Pier but I conquered death and the grave. Hallelujah!", I exclaimed. Then I heard the voice of a teacher in the hallway, "Yes! It's true! I was driving behind her from Drax Hall and as I drove passed the corner at Mystic Mountain, I saw the silver car overtaking the line of traffic in her lane and wondered if the driver was deliberately driving into all of us." She then explained to them how it unfolded.

I was looking forward to living with my husband in the United States. The days of travelling back and forth were over, and we were now planning how we would spend the rest of our lives together. We were excited about this new accomplishment. He was preparing to come home in another two weeks, and I was busy stocking up on the things that he loved. In the blink of an eye, all those plans were altered by unforeseen circumstances.

That Saturday afternoon, I did not go back to church because my husband had called me just as I came home for lunch. We spoke for a long time. Each time we ended our conversation, he called again, and we laughed and talked for another few minutes. Later that night, he called me again, but instead of speaking, he began to play his guitar. I reminded him of the days when he played at church during our teenage years, and we laughed about it. He played it for a long time: no singing, just serenading me with its harmony until I fell asleep.

The next morning, I awoke early and called him, expecting to hear his usual cheerful voice. It was not his voice I heard on the other end. Instead, it was the voice of a female paramedic, telling me that my husband was found at home unresponsive, and was on his way to the hospital. Shockwaves ran through my body as I quickly called my prayer partners to pray.

While we were praying, my phone rang. The voice at the other end said,

"They tried their best to save him, but he didn't make it."

This was the straw that broke the camel's back. I often tap into my memory to recall the sequence of events that followed, but without success, so I leave it to your imagination. One thing I know for sure is that within a few hours that Sunday, I was on the next flight to the United States, only to be told that he succumbed to cardiac arrest.

I felt myself sinking deeper into the dungeon as the days turned into weeks and months. I finally felt like throwing in the towel as the devil tried to show me that God could have saved him and He didn't. As I tried to search for answers, I knew this was another test of my faith. But this time, I was too weak to fight back spiritually. My world was now empty.

For a while, my faith in God grew weaker. I couldn't pray anymore because I felt like God had let me down. I became withdrawn, not thinking much of the future anymore. I just wanted my husband and lover back. I was haunted by flashbacks of my journey through "the Valley of Weeping", and wondered how I survived that calamity. I was in a world by myself. Tears were now my unspoken language. In the distance, I saw "the Valley of No Return", but didn't care much if I was heading that direction or not.

The spirit of depression was approaching, and I knew that this was more negative energy, so I had to be strong to resist the mood swings that ensued. Fortunately, my young grandchildren were around me to create laughter and fun, which minimized the effects of this disorder.

As the battle grew fiercer, my faith grew stronger because I knew I had God by my side. I just needed to tap into the wisdom, knowledge and understanding of the spiritual realm. I could only do this with the word of God. God is a God of impossibility and a God of miracles. He makes a way when there seems to be no other way. I gave the LORD my battles and worshiped Him incessantly. Surprisingly, I still maintained a normal life, although I was heart-broken. Looking back, it's hard to imagine how I maintained a healthy lifestyle throughout that dilemma, but God provided angels in my life to row my boat through the storm. We are told in Deuteronomy 28:12 that the LORD will open the heavens, the storehouse of His bounty, to send rain on our land in season and to bless all the work of our hands. We will be so blessed that we will lend to many nations, but will borrow from no one. As I won battle after battle, I knew then that my season of drought was only temporary because God had ended it. The autumn rains were now filling my pools with blessings from above.

As I reflect on my past, I am reminded that the weapons of our warfare are not carnal, but mighty through God to the pulling down of strongholds. (2 Corinthians 10:4 KJV). There are times when we are engaged in spiritual warfare and we don't even understand it. This warfare cannot be fought with weapons of the world like knives, swords or guns. The means to an end is spiritual. The means by which we manage our spiritual battle are spiritual. Our weapon that we use to manage this warfare is the word of God, the sword of the spirit, which is not carnal but are of a spiritual nature and have their effects on our mind and heart. They are both offensive and defensive because they serve to protect us and to refute the darts of the wicked. When we draw strength from God's word, we are equipped with a mighty force and power to pull down strongholds.

We also need the nine graceful attributes of the Fruit of the Spirit (love, joy, peace, longsuffering, kindness, goodness, faithfulness, gentleness, and self-control) to live in accordance with the Holy Spirit (Galatians 5:22-23 NKJV). We need to transform our personality by arming ourselves with the full armor of God so that we can stand against the evil schemes of our adversaries. After we have done that, we should stand firm with the belt of truth buckled around our waist, with the breastplate of righteousness in place, and our feet fitted with the readiness that comes from the gospel of peace. Then we are ready to take up the shield of faith, which we need to extinguish the fiery darts of the wicked. We must put on the helmet of salvation and take up the sword of the spirit, which is the word of God, and march out in prayer. We are now prepared for the spiritual warfare that is eminent; and as long as we allow God to lead and we follow, we will be more than conquerors through Him who loved us.

As I continue to meditate on the word of God, I gain strength spiritually; and I am no longer afraid, because of pride, to tell others of what the LORD has done for me. Many people will be hearing this story for the first time, as it's the LORD's will for me to share it because He has restored and blessed me abundantly after these trying times.

Prayer

―――※《◉》※―――

Heavenly Father, I thank You for being my strength and shield on the battlefield. Thank You for giving me the strength and courage to pull down the strongholds around me. Thank You for overturning every plan of the enemy. By Your power, I was able to trample upon the serpents and scorpions in my path. I plead the blood of Jesus over every problem affecting me. Let Your blood encircle me as a mark of protection. I hold it as a shield against every stubborn situation in my life. May You remove doubt, fear and discouragement; and give me the confidence to walk out in victory. I pray that You bind every spirit of infirmity, poverty, stagnation, sabotage, delay and confusion; and give us peace. I pray that You will supply our needs from Your resources in Glory. In Jesus' name, amen.

MARCHING INTO VICTORY

I completed my period of self-examination with humility, and was now prepared for a spiritual battle. As I remembered hearing people say, "They have the patience of Job", I reflected on his suffering and recognized that all was going well for him; but in spite of his wealth, his greatness and his faith in God, he lost everything, including his health. All this happened because God allowed it, knowing Job's strength of character and faith in Him. I was at the point in my life where I had to seek more of God so that my present situation would not impact my health negatively. Job's story gave me strength, and it encouraged me to embark upon a series of fasting and prayer.

First, I realized that I needed a more effective prayer life. I reflected on the story of Daniel and his petition to God. Like Daniel, I did not ask God to act in my own interest, but to act according to His will. I wanted more grace, favour, mercy and compassion.

Our spiritual life is an ongoing progression; and there are going to be hard times, evil influences and unfortunate encounters. But these obstacles can be overcome with good. The darkest part of the night is broken by the gleam of sunrise. So, in the depths of despair and in the midst of temptation, God will restore us.

Those who have ever travelled on a train will agree that once you board it, you are unable to see what is ahead. When it goes through a dark tunnel, we may become fearful, but we don't throw away the ticket and jump off. Instead, we sit still and trust the engineer. It's the same way God expects us to trust Him, no matter how rough our situation gets.

Daniel's story shows us that the first step of spiritual activity which will eventually set us free is embedded in the words, "Daniel set his face to the LORD God in fasting and prayer." This simple move could be the beginning to a series of spiritual encounters in our lives which will position us on the road to freedom and restoration. The scripture in Philippians 4:6 asks us not to be anxious about anything, but in every situation, by prayer and petition, with thanksgiving, present our request to God.

Daniel began with fasting and prayer, and that's exactly how we should begin fighting our spiritual battles. Daniel did not become complacent in his predicament. Instead, he focused on the LORD, who he expected to deliver Israel from seventy years of captivity in Babylon.

I was not deterred by the fact that in response to Daniel's prayer, God had sent His messenger back to Daniel, but the angel was stopped by the prince of the Persian kingdom. After wrestling with him and being detained for twenty-one days, Michael the Archangel came to help him. The Bible states that our struggles are not against flesh and blood; but against the rulers of darkness, against the power and authority of this dark world, and against the forces of evil in the spiritual realm. The LORD answered Daniel's prayer with honesty: "The city will be rebuilt... but there is work to be done in rebuilding it."

Sometimes, when we are getting out of the valley, we have to rebuild some things. It might be our reputation, our home, or our life. However, we are comforted by the fact that the LORD also walked this road before; and through His own power, He fought and defeated the same spiritual forces of evil.

I had never done more than a one-day fast before, but I conducted the necessary research and embarked on a 3-day dry fast, a 7-day fast, and then a 14-day fast. I secured a backup force of prayer partners, believing that God is still in control of my life. After successfully completing the 14-day fast, breakthrough and deliverance manifested in my entire household. God's grace and favour came in different forms. The persons in close contact received their share of blessings from God. God provided the helpers in my life to bridge the financial gaps until my own finances were released. May God continually bless these folks exceedingly, and replenish their stocks in abundance.

BREAK THE CHAINS

If we view Life's journey as a vehicle, we will realize that the road is not always smooth. We experience potholes and sometimes get a flat tire, or even get caught in a thunderstorm. We will not reach our destination if we stop the car and decide not to go any further. We have to change the tire and keep moving forward. Our experiences on the road to success or prosperity allow us to become stronger as our faith and reliance on God strengthen.

He makes us the head and not the tail. He says in Joel 2:25 that He will restore the years that the locust, the cankerworm, the caterpillar, and the palmerworm had eaten. He is in control of our life; and He expects us to take control of our situation, activate our faith and believe in him. We have to believe in ourselves too, and think outside the box. Think about the positive things that could have happened if we were not in this present situation. Our adversaries want to see us go down, and we have to prove them wrong. We have to break the chains, tear down the barriers that hold us down, and free ourselves.

Our mind is powerful, and we have to force ourselves to walk away from negativity and think positively. Only we can set ourselves free from the circumstances that hold us in captivity. If we don't try to break the chains, our minds may become so conditioned to being held captive that even when we are freed, it will take some time to realize that we are really free. We often become so complacent and accustomed to self-pity that when we are freed, we fail to make progress. We need to believe in ourselves and avoid comparing ourselves to others. We have to be willing to pick up the pieces, move on and leave the past behind.

When I realized that my marriage was irretrievable, I didn't get stuck in self-pity. I loved my husband very much, but I loved myself more. While I was hoping for a peaceful resolution that would provide permanent contentment, I buried my pride, maintained an open mind, and walk away when it didn't get any better. I didn't think I couldn't make it on my own. Instead, I fasted and prayed to God for direction. I didn't tell Him what I wanted Him to do. Instead, I approached Him with an open mind; and asked Him to do everything according to His will, and I will be satisfied with the outcome.

While I prayed, I put a contingency plan in place. I began to ask myself questions: "What can I do if this doesn't work out? Will I have to start all over again?" The scripture encourages us to cast our cares upon the Lord for He cares for us. There are times when in order to move ahead, we have to cut ties with persons around us. They become extra baggage or pessimists filled with doubts and self-pity; persons who, instead of being positive, remain negative regardless. Sometimes, unknown to us, they get involved in activities that are contrary to God's will.

Prayer

———⟫((◉))⟪———

Heavenly Father, You have been my dwelling place in all generations. From everlasting to everlasting, You are God. Draw me closer to You, LORD, and help me to live by Your word and not by my feelings. Thank You for leading, guiding and protecting me every step of the way. May Your presence continue to be with me. LORD, You have not given us a spirit of fear, but of power and of love, and of a sound mind. My destiny is in Your hands; so I pray that you nullify every writing, agreement or covenant against my work. In the name of Jesus, amen.

BEING AN OVERCOMER

Sometimes, we are so distraught and so burdened that even when our chains are broken and we are expected to move to another level, we appear to be stuck in our situations. This happens sometimes when we hold on to our past. We may blame others instead of evaluating ourselves. We may also be held back because of guilt from past mistakes, or because of fear.

When we experience breakthroughs from our present circumstances, we need to leave our past behind and march boldly and confidently into the future. Steve Maraboli's statement, "My past has not defined me, destroyed me, deterred me, or defeated me; it has only strengthened me", resonates with me as I reflect on the perils of my past and acknowledge how much I have exhibited the strength of a woman. There is no need to be a slave to fear anymore because we are God's children. His word tells us in Isaiah 41:10: "Fear not, for I am with thee: be not dismayed, for I am your God; I will strengthen you; yes, I will help you; I will uphold you with my righteous right hand." (NKJV) Whenever we feel afraid, we need to trust God more.

In trying to climb out of our "valleys", we find ourselves making choices or decisions, and we need to ask for his guidance. We also have to be careful not to get ourselves adapted to our "valley environment" so much that we change locations but still remain in that valley because of complacency. If we do, we may lack the willpower to move forward. If we tell ourselves that we can't do it, then we would be placing limitations on ourselves. Our thoughts are powerful; and if we think that we are a loser, we will eventually be a loser.

One of the poems by Jimmy Dean that I recited as a child went like this: "I can't change the direction of the wind, but I can adjust my sails to always reach my destination." I'm not my own; I belong to Jesus, so we should rely on Him to lead the way. He bled and died on Calvary; and His words, "It is finished", symbolize the end to all the negative encounters we are likely to have in life — things that may stand between us and our destiny. His death and subsequent resurrection have boosted our faith in the Christian belief that we can do all things through Christ who strengthens us.

When God allows us to overcome the "valley experiences", we must boldly say goodbye to depression, fear, anxiety, ill health, poverty, grief, and any other negative feeling we may have accommodated on our journey. As God's restoration takes place, we take on a new status. We become overcomers preparing ourselves to receive a double portion of His blessings. In all things, we are more than conquerors through Him who loved us. In spite of all the tribulations, despair, shame, and embarrassment we have been through, we are now saved by grace through faith. God has promised us that the one who is victorious, will get the right to sit with Him on His throne. (Revelation 3:21) (NIV) My blessings were somewhere on the horizon, but I had to be humbled enough to be able to appreciate them. I thank God for opening up the windows of Heaven to pour His blessings on me.

Sometimes, we work hard at our jobs but are denied the promotion we deserve because our supervisors, employers or managers are subjective in appraising us. Sometimes, we are the victims of various abuses in our relationships, and we do our best to make them work; but we still have to walk away when they don't. We often think life is unfair and wonder if God is still watching over us when things go wrong. We have to learn to use the stones that are thrown at us to build bridges to climb out of our situation. When God rescues us from the valley situation, we need to let go of the weight that so easily beset us and accept our present condition. We have to empty our vessels in order for them to be refilled. There are times when we have to clean our vessels too, because we cannot put new wine into old bottles. They will break, and the wine will run out. When we put new wine in new bottles, both the wine and the bottles are preserved.

King David was a man of clear contrasts. He experienced how humbling it was to be a shepherd boy, and how prestigious it was to reign over a nation. He experienced major triumphs and bitter defeats. He sought after God, but he also suffered immense guilt and pain from living immorally. When we read his Psalms, we can conclude that he was sometimes hopeful, and at other times, in despair. Yet, through it all, he continued to trust in God, he respected God's sovereign power, had confidence in God's timeline, and depended on God for deliverance. He too wanted to leave his past behind and march forward into victory, both spiritually and temporally; so he asked God to create in him a clean heart and renew a right spirit within him. (Psalm 51:10)

When we need a new beginning in any area of our life, we need to ask God to make us a new creation, a brand-new man. We need to believe that old things are passed away, and all things have become new. The scripture tells us that if any man is in Christ, he is a new creature. Old things are passed away; and behold all things are become new. (2 Corinthians 5:17) (KJV) In order to be overcomers, we have to make our relationship with God a priority, and develop an intimacy with him through prayer and the study of His word. Only then we will be able to enjoy the newness of life.

When God is about to bless us, we have to prepare ourselves to receive it. This portion of our journey should not be taken lightly, or taken for granted. We have to speak boldly to our situation because words are powerful. If we need breakthrough, deliverance, healing, etc., we should proclaim it daily over our lives and seal that proclamation in the name of Jesus. When God changes our story, there should be a transformation taking place where we shed the old and put on the new. We are now at a level where we are exchanging beauty for ashes—let go of the ashes and accept thebeauty.

FROM GLORY TO GLORY

As I pen the last chapter of this book, I do so with a thankful heart. Looking back on my journey, I am reminded that if God leads us to it, He will take us through it. His mercy kept me, and I didn't let go. God is sovereign because He is in absolute control of the entire universe. He reigns supreme and owns everything in Heaven and Earth. His resources are unlimited, and everything He has done or has given to us is for His glory alone. He is worthy to receive glory, honour and praise. We are called to submit ourselves to Him, and to act according to His will.

It is important for us to maintain a relationship with Him. This relationship goes beyond accepting Him as LORD and Saviour. It means interacting with Him on a daily basis, and allowing Him to order our steps in our everyday life. It is God's desire that we may behold His glory. The LORD tells us in Haggai 2:5-9, that we should not fear, for He is with us. He will fill our house with glory. He promises that the glory of this present house will be greater than the glory of the former house, and in this place He will give peace. God is ready to move us from glory to glory.

Paul sums up our entire Christian life when he said, "And we all, who with unveiled face, contemplate the LORD's glory, are being transformed into His image with ever-increasing glory, which comes from the LORD, who is the spirit." (2 Corinthians 3:18) (NIV). When we sin, we fall short of God's glory, but He is always willing and able to forgive us. He is an awesome God and is worthy of our praise. Now that we are overcomers, living from glory to glory, we are expected to share the good news of salvation.

David implores us to give thanks unto the LORD, for He is good, for His mercy endures forever. He said, "Oh, that men would praise the LORD for His goodness, and for His wonderful works to the children of men!" Psalm 107:31 (KJV) We serve a Mighty God and His mercy is unchanging. It endures forever and ever.

GOD'S GRACE AND FAVOUR

Grace is when we get what we don't expect or deserve. God has saved us and called us to a holy life—not because of anything we have done, but because of His own purpose and grace. We don't deserve God's favour, but because of His unconditional love for us, we receive His grace and forgiveness in spite of our past. We are given a chance to start afresh, pick up the pieces if we may, and move on. We might not be perfect, but remember, He has forgiven us. He promises that His grace is sufficient to keep us, so we should not be tempted to go back to the mistakes of our past.

We should always cultivate good thoughts and remain positive or optimistic as much as possible. The grief of the past sometimes clouds our minds, but the sun is a daily reminder that we too can rise again from the darkness of our past. The dark clouds of doubt hanging over us can be replaced with confidence knowing that God is still in control. Our mind is like a magnet and will draw whatever we think about. If we think of success, we will attract success; if we think of problems, we attract problems; if we think of failure, we attract failure. So, let us learn to control our thoughts.

FAITH IN GOD

Faith shows the reality of what we constantly hope for, and it is the evidence of things we are unable to see (Hebrews 11: 1). It requires that we believe and trust in the LORD, for the Bible declares that without faith, it is impossible to please God. Our faith in God translates to the level of trust we have in Him.

There are many people today who are overcome by depression because they spend more time and energy focusing on their present circumstances instead of solutions to their problems. They are often so overwhelmed by their problems that they don't realize that the enemy is trying to steal their joy. This anxiety creates unnecessary weight that holds us back, and prevents us from moving forward. We need to understand that without faith, we cannot accomplish anything. We must develop an attitude of expectancy and relinquish any negative thoughts that may linger in our minds. The scripture declares, "Verily I say unto you, if you have faith as a grain of mustard seed, you shall say to this mountain, 'Remove hence to yonder place,' and it shall remove; and nothing shall be impossible unto you." (Matthew 17:20) We should be in a position to speak to our situation with confidence, believing that our words are powerful.

When we walk by faith, and not by sight, we enjoy an intimate relationship with God. Enoch's life exemplifies the walk of faith. He walked with God, and so he experienced a wonderful relationship with God. By faith, he was taken up so that he should not see death. His life pleased God so much that after more than three hundred years on Earth, he was translated to heaven without encountering death. God delights in our walk with Him. He delights in our praise and worship.

PUTTING GOD FIRST

We must put God first in our lives if we want to successfully jump over the hurdles that rise before us as we journey along. The Bible declares that we live in a way that proves we belong to the God who calls us unto His Kingdom and glory (1 Thessalonians 2:12).

Once we have surrendered or submitted to God's will, we should tap into God's powerful resources. The scripture tells us that everything comes from Him, exists by His power, and is intended for His glory (Romans 11:36). Some people have money, family, friends, you name it; but they still feel unfulfilled. They cannot find fulfilment in life until they begin to live by God's power and for His glory, working according to His will. Rick Warren created an acrostic showing the five things in which we need to put God **FIRST:**

"Finances: If you want God to bless your finances, even during difficult seasons, you must tithe. Sorry! There's no alternative.

Interests: Give God first consideration in your decision. Put Him first in your career, your hobbies and your recreation.

Relationships: Put Him first in your family, marriage and your friendships.

Schedule: Give Him the first part of everyday. Say to Him every morning, "God, if I don't get anything else done today, I just want to love you more and know you a little better."

Troubles: You need to turn to God first when you have a problem. Prayer should never be your last resort; it should be your first choice."

My desire is to put God first in my life, and try my best to let His will be done in my life. I will join with Paul, when on his third missionary journey, he said, "However, I consider my life worth nothing to me; my only aim is to finish the race and complete the task the LORD Jesus has given me—the task of testifying to the good news of God's grace." Acts 20:24 (NIV)

Prayer

———⊰⟨⟨◉⟩⟩⊱———

Heavenly Father, thank You for your grace and favour on my life. Your blessings are new every morning. LORD, walk with me because I am nothing without Your presence. I am sanctified to be in Your presence; I am justified to be in Your presence. My Redeemer, let Your grace reach out to me. Continue to open up supernatural doors for me. Fill my house with Your glory; for Your word says that the glory of this present house will be greater that the glory of the former house, and You will give us Your peace.

Give me more strength in my weakness; give me faith in moments of doubt and fear. Give me the power to overcome the challenges. Give me the courage to proclaim Your word with freedom and boldness so that others will be led to glorify You. Stay with me as seek more of You. Today, I pray like Jabez that You will bless me and enlarge my territory. Be with me in all that I do, and keep me from all trouble, harm and pain. In Jesus' name, amen.

CONCLUSION

My readers, I thank you for travelling with me as I share these experiences with you. It has been a long climb to the mountain top but God kept His promise that He will supply my needs according to His riches in glory in Christ Jesus. Philippians 4:19 (KJV) To God be the glory, great things He has done. I am now retired from forty years of successful unbroken service as an educator and God has enlarged my territory. My journey has reached a plateau where I am now my own boss and my steps are still ordered by God. Most of my time is dedicated to motivating others and sharing my testimony of God's grace and mercy.

I implore you to be brave and live the life of your dreams according to your vision and allow God to fulfill His purpose in you. Never allow the opinions and expectations of others to limit the scope of your success. Disassociate yourselves from coward, pessimistic people. You can interact with them, maintain a good rapport, and not be easily influenced. We often create our own problems by becoming friendly with people we should just greet and pass quickly. We need to choose our role models wisely because successful people build up each other. Those who aspire to greatness motivate, inspire and help others. People who are unsuccessful usually hate, grudge, demotivate, blame, make excuses and complain.

Let your passion for growth and success drive you. According to Steve Maraboli, "If we hang out with chickens, we are going to cluck and if we hang out with eagles, we are going to fly." We can only fly when we identify the unnecessary baggage pulling us down and rid ourselves of them. When you are bombarded by problems or challenges, be like the eagle that soars because it focuses on its goal instead of the obstacles in its path. Whenever it encounters a storm it uses the negative energy to soar even higher. The eagle will never challenge its enemy in its comfort zone or on the ground. Instead, it changes the battleground by picking up its foe and taking it into familiar territory in the sky where its assailant becomes powerless. So, take your battles to the spiritual realm through fasting and prayer where God can fight them for you. Then and only then, will you guarantee a complete victory.

Let us continue to lift our faith and put our trust in God. He is a miracle working God and a God of impossibility. If He did it for me, He will do it for you too. He is able to fight our battles and lift our burdens. All He wants in return, is our sacrifices of praise. May God fill your hearts with His love and His peace. God bless you. Shalom!

Prayer of Thanksgiving

LORD, I thank You for the gift of life.
For Your forgiveness of my sins.
For Your grace and mercy, which kept
me safe and secure throughout my journey.
For the relationship that I have with You.
For taking me safely through the rough places.
For Your word, which provided light for my path.
For providing peace in the midst of the storm.
For providing comfort on difficult days.
For the wisdom to know the truth.
For the knowledge to understand the
difference between good and evil.
For Your unconditional love,
and for Your Holy Spirit.
Thank You for family and friends who helped me in various ways.
Help me to live and work according to Your will.
LORD, I have finally told my story in the best way I possibly could.
I trust that it is done according to Your will.
I surrender my all to You, withholding nothing,
As I await my next assignment.
In the name of Jesus, Amen.

MY SPIRITUAL ROADMAP

Psalm 23

The LORD is my Shepherd; I shall not want.

He maketh me to lie down in green pastures: He leadeth me beside still waters.

He restoreth my soul: He leadeth me in the paths of righteousness for

His name's sake.

Yea, though I walk through the valley of the shadow of death, I will fear no evil: for thou art with me; thy rod and thy staff they comfort me.

Thou preparest a table before me in the presence of mine enemies: Thou anointest my head with oil; my cup runneth over.

Surely goodness and mercy shall follow me all the days of my life: and I will dwell in the house of the LORD for ever.

Psalm 23

The LORD's Prayer

Our Father who art in Heaven,
Hallowed be thy Name,
Thy Kingdom come.
Thy will be done on earth as it is in Heaven.
Give us this day our daily bread.
And forgive us our trespasses,
As we forgive those who trespass against us.
And lead us not into temptation,
But deliver us from evil.
For thine is the Kingdom,
And the power and the glory,
For ever and ever, Amen.

Psalm 46

God is our refuge and strength, an ever-present help in trouble.
Therefore, we will not fear, though the earth give way
And the mountains fall into the heart of the sea,
Though its waters roar and foam
And the mountains quake with their surging.
There is a river whose streams make glad the city of God,
The holy place where the Most High dwells.
God is within her, she will not fall;
God will help her at break of day.
Nations are in uproar, kingdoms fall;
He lifts his voice, the earth melts.
The LORD Almighty is with us,
The God of Jacob is our fortress.
Come and see what the LORD has done,
The desolations He has brought on the earth.
He makes wars cease to the ends of the earth.
He breaks the bow and shatters the spear;
He burns the shields with fire.
He says, "Be still, and know that I am God;
I will be exalted among the nations,
I will be exalted in the earth."
The LORD Almighty is with us;
the God of Jacob is our fortress.

Psalm 27

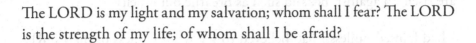

The LORD is my light and my salvation; whom shall I fear? The LORD is the strength of my life; of whom shall I be afraid?

When the wicked, even mine enemies and my foes, came upon me to eat up my flesh, they stumbled and fell.

Though an host should encamp against me, my heart shall not fear: though war should rise against me, in this will I be confident.

One thing have I desired of the LORD, that will I seek after; that I may dwell in the house of the LORD all the days of my life, to behold the beautify of the LORD, and to enquire in His temple.

For in the time of trouble He shall hide me in His pavilion: in the secret of his tabernacle shall He hide me; He shall set me up upon a rock.

And now shall mine head be lifted up above mine enemies round about me: therefore will I offer in His tabernacle sacrifices of joy; I will sing, yea, I will sing praises unto the LORD.

Hear, O LORD, when I cry with my voice: have mercy also upon me, and answer me.

When thou saidst, Seek ye my face; my heart said unto thee, Thy face, LORD, will I seek.

Hide not thy face far from me; put not thy servant away in anger: thou hast been my help; leave me not, neither forsake me, O God of my salvation.

When my father and my mother forsake me, then the LORD will take me up.

Teach me thy way, O LORD, and lead me in a plain path, because of mine enemies.

Deliver me not over unto the will of mine enemies: for false witnesses are risen up against me, and such as breathe out cruelty.

I had fainted, unless I had believed to see the goodness of the LORD in the land of the living.

Wait on the LORD: be of good courage, and he shall strengthen thine heart: wait, I say, on the LORD.

Psalm 91

He that dwelleth in the secret place of the most High shall abide under the shadow of the Almighty.

I will say of the LORD, He is my refuge and fortress: my God, in Him will I trust.

Surely He shall deliver thee from the snare of the fowler, and from the noisome pestilence.

He shall cover thee with His feathers, and under His wings shalt thou trust: His truth shall be thy shield and buckler.

Thou shalt not be afraid for the terror by night; nor for the arrow that flieth by day;

Nor for the pestilence that walketh in darkness; nor for the destruction that wasteth at noonday.

A thousand shall fall at thy side, and ten thousand at thy right hand; but it shall not come nigh thee.

Only with thine eyes shalt thou behold and see the reward of the wicked.

Because thou hast made the LORD, which is thy refuge, even the most High, thy habitation;

There shall no evil befall thee, neither shall any plague come nigh thy dwelling.

For He shall give His angels charge over thee, to keep thee in all thy ways.

They shall bear thee up in their hands, lest thou dash thy foot against a stone.

Thou shalt tread upon the lion and the adder: the young lion and the dragon shalt thou trample under feet.

Because He hath set His love upon me, therefore will I deliver him: I will set him on high, because he hath known my name.

He shall call upon me, and I will answer Him: I will be with him in trouble; I will deliver him, and honour him.

With long life will I satisfy him, and shew him my salvation.

INSPIRATIONAL QUOTES

The following inspirational quotes provided me with strength as I travelled through the various valleys. I hope you will also be inspired as you read them:

O LORD, my God, how excellent is Your name in all the earth? You are compassionate and gracious. You are my stronghold in times of trouble and my shelter in every storm. You blot out my transgressions and supply my needs. You are able to do immeasurably more than I ask or imagine. LORD, I worship You.

Gertrude Flynn-White

God's mercies are new every day for those who need a fresh start in any area of life. Let go of the old and receive the new blessing that God has in store for you. Trust Him, believe His promise, and receive your blessing. Gertrude Flynn-White

---

Relax in the peaceful presence of God. Let His unconditional love flow into your spirit, soul and mind. Allow the LORD to fill your thoughts with spiritual food as you focus on Him. Gertrude Flynn-White

---

Never run away from the problems of your past. They will chase you into your future. Face them with confidence, for God is bigger than every problem. Gertrude Flynn-White

---

And this is my prayer: that your love may abound more and more in knowledge and depth of insight, so that you may be able to discern what is best and may be pure and blameless for the day of Christ, filled with the fruit of righteousness that comes through Jesus Christ—to the glory and praise of God. (Philippians 1:9 and 11) NIV

For it is God who works in you to will and to act according to His good purpose. Do everything without complaining or arguing, so that you may become blameless and pure, children of God, without fault in a crooked and depraved generation, in which you shine like stars in the universe as you hold out the word of life—in order that I may boast on the day of Christ that I did not run or labour for nothing. Philippians 2:13-16 NIV

The LORD is my strength and song, and He has become my salvation.(Exodus 15:2) KJV

For God has not given us a spirit of fear, but of power and of love and of a sound mind.
2 Timothy 1:7 NKJV

And we know that in all things God works for the good of those who love him, who have been called according to His purpose.
Romans 8:28 NIV

The LORD is my strength and my shield; my heart trusts
in Him, and I am helped. My heart leaps for joy and
I will give thanks to him in song.
Psalm 28: 7 NIV

But let patience have its perfect work, that you may
be perfect and complete, lacking nothing.
James 1:4 NKJV

Consider it pure joy, my brothers and sisters, whenever you face trials of
many kinds, because you know that the testing of your faith produces
perseverance. Let perseverance finish its work so that you may be mature
and complete, not lacking anything. If any of you lacks wisdom, you
should ask God, who gives generously to all without finding fault, and it
will be given to you. But when you ask, you must believe and not doubt,
because the one who doubts is like a wave of the sea, blown and tossed
by the wind, That person should not expect to receive anything from the
LORD. Blessed is the one who perseveres under trial because, having
stood the test, that person will receive the crown of life that the LORD
has promised to those who love Him. (James 1:2, 3, 4, 5, 6 7 and 12) NIV

Be strong and courageous. Do not be afraid; do not be discouraged,
for the LORD your God will be with you wherever you go.
Joshua 1:9 NIV

Do not let any unwholesome talk come out of your mouths, but
only what is helpful for building others up according to their
needs, that it may benefit those who listen. (Ephesians 4:29) NIV

ABOUT THE AUTHOR

A powerful, inspiring and interesting story of triumph.

On a journey of accomplishment overshadowed by challenges and adversity, Gertrude invites readers into her world as she gives an account of how her strong faith in God helped her to triumph over adversity.

She refused to allow her humble beginning to limit or define her destiny. Using captivating experiences, backed by Biblical characters who had their own valley encounters, and a peep into her prayer life, she shares her story.

In spite of the struggles, disappointment, grief and loss, Gertrude maintained a close relationship with God. She showed how her faith helped her bypass the stresses of life and overcome the challenges.

Her strong will to rise above the circumstances that were intended to dehumanize her, allowed her to experience the supernatural power of God. She relied on Him for inner peace, strength, protection and direction as she tried to beat the odds and fulfill her purpose.

This book will encourage and empower you to accept the things you cannot change, activate your faith to trust God as He is in control of your life.

You can follow me on:
https://www.facebook.com/myvalleyxperience.baca (Facebook)
@myvalleyxperience (Instagram)
https://myvalleyxperience.com (Website)

NOTES

Printed in the United States
By Bookmasters